What is 'It'?

T0341076

Paula Nagel

Illustrated by Gary Bainbridge

Routledge
Taylor & Francis Group

LONDON AND NEW YORK

First published 2017
by Routledge
2 Park Square, Milton Park, Abingdon, Oxon OX14 4RN

and by Routledge
711 Third Avenue, New York, NY 10017

Routledge is an imprint of the Taylor & Francis Group, an informa business

British Library Cataloguing-in-Publication Data
A catalogue record for this book is available from the British Library

Library of Congress Cataloging-in-Publication Data
A catalog record for this book has been requested.

ISBN: 978 1 90930 178 8 (pbk)
ISBN: 978 1 31517 519 5 (ebk)

Typeset in Univers Light Condensed
by Moo Creative (Luton)

Visit the eResources: www.routledge.com/9781909301788

MIX
Paper from
responsible sources
FSC® C013604

Printed and bound by CPI Group (UK) Ltd, Croydon, CR0 4YY

3

She doesn't understand!
That makes two of us.
Does she really think I want to feel like this?!

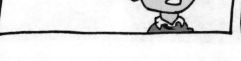

So it's not your homework or Miss Corbett or Lucy or your sister...

And your mum wasn't mad at you this morning...

Nah... She was too busy going off to buy flowers...

She's going to put them on Tony's grave today.

oh...

But I feel really upset anyhow.
It's stupid...
It's been a year since he died, so how come I feel so rubbish?

Big feelings come and go...

Sometimes we know immediately where those feelings come from...

But sometimes they are all muddled up and it's hard to understand them.

Sometimes big feelings happen when you think about people and things you miss...

Or things you used to do but don't do any more...

What is 'It' Workbook 2

Let's talk about ... sadness and loss

Here's Sam to share some of the things he learned about sadness and loss.

It's normal to feel big, not-so-good feelings from time to time. Sadness can be a big, not-so-good feeling.

Lots of things can make us feel sad.

Can you think of times when you felt any big feelings such as sadness? Draw or write about them on the weather clouds below.

Words that people might use when they feel sad include ...

It's normal to feel sad for lots of different reasons, like when we've heard an upsetting story or if we fall out with our friends.

We might feel sad and unsettled when we have experienced some kind of loss, such as losing something special, or missing someone or something.

Some of my friends told me they felt sad when they moved to a new home or school, when their parents split up, or when their pet died.

I felt really sad when my cousin Tony died, and when I remembered that time.

Sadness can be a big feeling. Experiencing loss can cause lots of different feelings too. These big feelings can affect your behaviour.

Look back at my story and see how sadness affected my behaviour.
Can you find a time when ...

- I couldn't concentrate?

- I felt agitated and angry?

- My big feelings stopped me doing something I would usually do?

Can you spot any other times when sad feelings affected my behaviour?

But I was in bed really early last night....

But big feelings such as sadness can be helpful too.

Feeling sad can help us to heal and recover after a difficult time or event.

When other people notice that we are feeling sad, it can signal that we need some support.

Sharing our feelings of sadness with other people can help us cope.

In my story, Jay noticed my behaviour and wondered how I was feeling, so he took time to talk to me about it.

Look back and see if you can spot how Jay helped me to understand my big feelings.

Big feelings such as sadness can come and go.

Some of my big feelings didn't stay the same and kept changing.

I was sad when I remembered my cousin.

I felt angry when people kept telling me to smile.

I felt guilty when I forgot what day it was and I started having fun.

Do a daily weather check.

Big feelings and emotions can change - just like the weather.

Notice the sky today - what can you see?
White fluffy clouds? Grey misty clouds?
Big black clouds? Sun? Rain? A bit of both?

Draw or write about the weather today in the spaces below.

When you feel sad, it might sometimes seem as if there is a big black cloud following you around.

This cloud might block out the sun for a while.

But, just like the weather, your feelings won't stay the same for ever.

They will change.

Do a daily weather check to notice your feelings and emotions.

What is your emotional weather report today?
Happy, sad, or a bit of both?

Think about where you notice big feelings, such as sadness, in your body.

Perhaps your stomach wobbles or you feel sick?

Do you feel hot or cold?

Do you breathe faster or does your chest feel tight?

Do your muscles tense or shake?

Do you notice it anywhere else?

Write an 'X' where you notice big feelings in your body.

If you're not sure where you notice big feelings such as sadness in your body, try to notice the next time you have a big feeling.

Sometimes it takes time for the weather to change and blow away the black clouds.

Sometimes it can take time for your big feelings to blow away.

Although we can't affect the weather outside, we can do things to notice and manage our feelings and mood.

Let's think about the things you can do to help you notice and manage your feelings.

Talking about your black cloud days can help to blow them away.

If you have lots of black cloud days it is good to talk about it.

In the story I talked about my feelings with my friend Jay, and with my teacher. They helped me t think about some of the reasons I had big feelings

They helped me to understand that feelings of sadness can affect my behaviour, and that feeling come and go.

This is normal.

Talk about how you feel
– especially when you have big feelings.

Keep a watchful eye on your emotional weather

Keep a diary to notice when your feelings change throughout the day or the week.

Notice the things that help you and try to do more of them.

My weather watch

Monday morning –

How I felt: Tired and couldn't concentrate.

What I was doing and thinking: Thinking about Tony and the flowers for his grave.

What helped: Joining in with Lucy at play time.

Monday lunch time

Monday afternoon

Monday home time

When you have big feelings such as sadness, try to **keep on doing the things you enjoy** ... even if you don't really feel like it!

What do you really enjoy doing?

Write them down or draw them in the spaces below.

If you experience loss – **try making a memory book or box**.

Fill it with things you remember about the person or things you liked to do together – think about pictures, stories, songs and activities.

Summary

Always remember, the weather doesn't stay the same for ever... and big feelings such as sadness will change too!

Remember big feelings such as sadness can help us recover, and signal to other people that we need their support. Noticing and sharing big feelings such as sadness can be helpful.

However, if your sad feelings start to affect you for a long time, you might need some more help.

Tell someone you trust how your big feelings are affecting you straight away.